The Art of Teaching
CLASSICAL BALLET

Woytek Lowski

The Art of Teaching
CLASSICAL BALLET

Woytek Lowski

DANCE BOOKS
CECIL COURT LONDON

Original title: *O nauczaniu Tańca Klasycznego*
Translated by Antonia Lloyd Jones

Published by
Dance Books Ltd
15 Cecil Court
London WC2N 4EZ
United Kingdom

in association with Maksymilian art publisher

A CIP catalogue record for this book
is available from the British Library

ISBN 1 85273 045 5

© 1998 Tomasz Kaczyński

Printed and bound in Great Britain by The Charlesworth Group,
Huddersfield, England, 01484 517077.

Editors: Josephine Jewkes, Tim Almaas
Cover design: Paweł Kamiński
Design: Sanjoy Roy

Contents

Illustrations

*This book is dedicated to
Rosella Hightower with gratitude,
to Elizabeth Anderton with admiration,
and to all my teachers with fond memories.*

Acknowledgements to Anna Paskevska and Wayne Stuarte.

*Many thanks to everyone who made this book possible, especially to
Catherine and Michael Jewkes. Thanks also to Josephine Jewkes
and Tim Almaas, whose enthusiasm and professionalism
contributed greatly to this book.*

Ballet is an expression of the very essence of life; it is the greatest physical and spiritual celebration. Dance is the union of time and space. Its limitations and transitory nature form the very nature of its beauty. It only exists in time and memory. One must constantly keep on seeking it out and rediscovering it. It is a never-ending search for a perfection to which one can only aspire in each successive performance.

Woytek Lowski

Foreword

Woytek Lowski has a unique contribution to make to the dance world. His presence in the studio inspires respect and affection. Woytek has successfully synthesised his experiences as a dancer in widely differing schools and styles to formulate his own meticulously constructed class. The class purifies the dancer's technique with its healthy and logical progression of exercises, always integrating elegant and harmonious ports de bras and épaulement. The 'curve of movement' is brought out in all its beauty. Woytek's class is always delivered with his own quiet brand of humour. A typical example from the first class he gave for the English National Ballet when we were on tour was the remark: 'It's not how much turn-out you have – it's how you hang on to what you've got.' This hit home while simultaneously raising a chuckle among tired dancers.

Woytek's contribution to the rehearsal studio is equally valuable. Dancers, whether male or female, inexperienced or well-established, look forward to probing sessions where every nuance of technique and interpretation may be explored. Woytek's wide cultural knowledge enables him to inspire us with images from film, opera, painting and sculpture, as well as with videos from his covetable collection of dance on film. He works with us to push back the boundaries of our own capabilities rather than imposing a rigid ideal from outside. This 'adaptability' is the mark of a generous artist.

In short, teaching is an art form and Woytek Lowski is a rare artist.

Josephine Jewkes

Woytek Lowski in Roland Petit's *La Rose malade.*

Apprenticeship of a stage coach driver
or How I became a ballet master

I don't remember when for the first time I visualised a future for myself as a teacher. I think the certainty that I would eventually become one must have taken root from my very first class as a thirteen–year-old student at the Warsaw State Ballet School. Prior to that time my ambition had been to become an actor, and to that end I had set about acquiring the necessary academic qualifications that would ensure my entry into the Warsaw State School of Acting when I reached the age of eighteen. However, rather than being a mere stepping-stone to the acting profession I felt my blood run faster as soon as the music started for the dance class, and I was hooked. I knew that my future lay in the dance world.

If I were going to be a dancer, then I had to be the best. Russian ballet films, guest appearances of artists from Leningrad and Moscow, and a visit to Warsaw by the American Ballet Theatre were all proof that I had a long way to go to reach the standard of other dancers. Thus my efforts to win a scholarship abroad became my most important goal. After almost two years of trying I was finally accepted by the Agrippina Vaganova School and the Kirov Theatre Ballet in Leningrad.

Fortune smiled on me again, and I was placed in the care of Alexander Pushkin, one of the most renowned teachers in the history of dance (Nureyev and Baryshnikov were among his pupils); also, it was just at that very time that a two-year course in the methodology of teaching classical dance was established. My teacher on this course was Olga Jordan, who has also gone down in history – the roles of Zarema in *The Fountain of Bakhchisaray* and Jeanne in *The Flames of Paris* were created for her. I had met this enchanting lady before in Warsaw, where she had taught for a year at the Warsaw Ballet School.

The set-up for my studies was ideal – morning lessons at school, later on with the theatre's soloists, classes in theory in the afternoon, and then evenings spent watching ballet performances in the theatre. My eyes and brain were endlessly bombarded with new images and new information, ever more frequently and more insistently sending signals to the rest of my body during the practical lessons afterwards, demanding greater discipline in the quest for perfection. And at the time the concept of perfection kept changing its meaning on an almost daily basis, getting further and further away the nearer I got, like the horizon.

I was twenty-one years old then, and hadn't yet thought what would happen to me once I had to leave the stage. Anyway, I kept noting down as many lessons as I could, both Pushkin's and those of all the other teachers, from the first to the very last class. It's hard for me to say now whether I did it to gain extra information to help me dance, or whether the teaching instinct was already making its demands on me.

My two years of study in Leningrad evidently brought results, for in Warsaw I was given the role of Basilio in *Don Quixote*, and at the competition in Varna I was awarded the silver medal. I left Varna convinced that I didn't have the right strength of nerve for competitions, and that they were more like contests for athletes than for artists.

The next result of my scholarship was the offer of a contract from Maurice Béjart, during the first performances in Warsaw of his Ballet of the Twentieth Century. My five years of working with this company was the period when my awareness as a dancer of a more modern, freer involvement of the body, arms and head in movement on stage was born and developed. Everything that had formerly been recognised as either correct or incorrect movement from the aesthetic point of view of the Vaganova school was now re-examined for its qualities of personal sincerity and expressiveness and whether those would communicate beyond the footlights or not. Béjart makes strict demands on his dancers to recognise the laws of the stage and to be deeply conscious of how movement on it is perceived by the audience.

As a future teacher, I could now choose from among the famous names and take part in the classes of the most renowned teachers in Paris. It was in

Béjart's company that I heard for the first time, 'that teacher is good because his classes "don't hurt" and every pas seems possible, but that teacher isn't, because it's hard to dance freely after one of his classes'. Until then I had always had the teacher assigned to me, and couldn't judge him because I had never had any choice or any scale of comparison.

During my first travels with the Ballet of the Twentieth Century I went to Europe's famous Rosella Hightower ballet school in Cannes. Meeting Rosella played a great, virtually landmark role in the forming of my personality as a ballet master. As a dancer I already knew how to move and how a pas should look, but I couldn't always repeat it in exactly the same way. Like sportsmen's bodies, dancers' bodies are extremely sensitive to the passage of time and to circumstances. Often even minor ailments cause a noticeable decline in quality of performance. My innate enthusiasm and strength-testing approach to the problems of dance were balanced out (and I am a Libran, after all) by Rosella's sensible, no-nonsense approach to the technique of ballet as an exact science. This meant that instead of moving in a whirl of persistent repetition without a pas succeeding, I had first to understand its mechanics and the reasons why it wasn't working for me. Only then could I work on it, eliminating mistakes in co-ordination, in order to be able to perform it at will in future and to repeat it, even under conditions which weren't always ideal.

My professional dictionary became enriched with ideas that were new to me: 'the body's centre of gravity and the conscious shift from one leg to the other in accordance with the laws of balance, and its dependence on the basis and axis of revolution'; the en dehors as 'a rotation in the hip joint' and not just the placement of the feet in five positions; 'the shock-absorption of low-ering oneself to the floor through a properly exercised metatarsus'; 'working in opposition', that is with the standing side of the body in opposition to the working leg side, using the floor as opposition to the force of gravity; and so on. In other words, Rosella taught me to think during my everyday work, and not just to rely solely on instinct or passive imitation of others.

After five years with Béjart I moved to Roland Petit's company, and from there to Boston ballet as their premier danseur, dancing all the major classics. This was a key period for me as an eventual ballet master. I became familiar,

3

not just in theory but in practice, with many different non-classical techniques and styles; without knowing these a dancer at the turn of the twenty-first century will have serious problems. The repertoire of most ballet companies in the world is beginning to be a collage of world-wide tradition along with the most interesting modern achievements in dance.

Boston, located near New York, gave me the chance to exercise, but at the same time to watch and learn from classes given by the greatest masters in that city. I took part in these classes at my own cost, and any dancer who pays for his classes always does his best not to waste his money. Thus too it was up to me to understand and to feel for myself why classes given by Maggie Black, David Howard and Stanley Williams were the most crowded.

With time, a limitation on the movement in my left hip joint prevented me from taking part in the company classes and forced me to work on my own. As I continued to perform on stage for another two years (in spite of my worsening state of health), the aim of these solitary exercises was to warm up with the minimum effort but the maximum result. This has also remained a tool in my work as a ballet master whose own arthritic hip has taught him the most effective, sensible way to take care of the health of others. At the same time I was reading every book I could get on kinetics and anatomy in relation to classical dance and to teaching it.

In this situation, leaving the stage was a relief for me, rather than a drama. The first person to give me a hand along this new road was my guru, Rosella Hightower. After several months' teaching work at her school I was showered with invitations from most of the world's major companies.

After three years of constant travel I got my first year-long contract from Mikhail Baryshnikov, then director of the American Ballet Theatre in New York. And it was there that one day after classes, as the usual day's rehearsals were beginning, that I suddenly found myself standing in front of Natalia Makarova and Baryshnikov as their ballet master for a rehearsal of *Other Dances*. This duet, to music by Chopin, was specially created for them by the great Jerome Robbins.

I am certain that in the United States time is dearer than in any other country and no one ever wastes it. So what could I, conducting this rehearsal of Robbins' ballet, have to offer Makarova, who had already been coached for the ballet by the choreographer himself? Aware that what great stars need above all is warm moral support, a boost of courage and correction of any slight technical errors (which in Baryshnikov's case was superfluous), I also understood that at that moment it was me who was the pupil and that I was being given a great opportunity to practice my new profession. And thus it has remained to this day; as I search for the solution to some problem I often ask myself the question, how would Natasha Makarova have danced this, or Cynthia Gregory, the brilliant Gelsey Kirkland, Martine van Hamel, or Fernando Bujones? In any rehearsal I try to create a calm atmosphere, suggesting certain improvements without shouting or forcing.

I learned a lot from these great stars, but it was also a time for looking my own limitations in the face, a time of coming to maturity. I regret, for instance, that I did not have the right musical education. It would now be very helpful in my work, and I would encourage all would-be teachers to include music studies in their education.

When one is a guest teacher one can manage fine with thirty pre-prepared lessons, repeating them in various different cities. When teaching the same company all the time, to avoid boring oneself and others, one must keep on developing and trying to make each lesson different, better, more interesting than the one before. In order to feel calm in front of a group of dancers and to meet up to their expectations, I prepare the lesson in a notebook and teach it from memory. I have been doing it like that for fifteen years now. Composing the lesson takes me at least two hours, but learning it by heart takes about ten minutes. I have hundreds of them written down. However, it's often the case that the ones from a few years ago don't appeal to me any more; often I can't see any sense in them at all, and I realise how my horizons are still shifting and my ideas developing.

The next important phase in my life as a ballet master was my collaboration with Valery Panov. Being a top-class dancing actor, as a choreographer he seems almost to use a chisel to compose his ballets, most of which are based on great works of world literature. With Panov I confirmed the conviction, which I already had from working with Béjart, that a dancer does not act by making faces. To be understood by the spectator in the back row his movements must be so expressive, generous, sincere and convincing that the character whom he is sculpting with his own muscles comes alive, three-dimensional and human in his experiences and conflicts.

Not long ago I began my forty-first year in the profession and my sixteenth as a teacher. For five years I have been working with English National Ballet (the former London Festival Ballet, founded in 1951 by Alicia Markova and Anton Dolin). At first I taught at the company's school, where I had the time and opportunity to try out many of my theories and ideas on my pupils.

More recently, working purely with the soloists of English National Ballet, preparing them mainly for roles in the great classical repertoire, before each rehearsal I ask myself a series of questions, in order to set my priorities within a chosen set of problems:

1. How much time do I have before the dancers with whom I am working go out on stage?
2. Are they managing mechanically; that is, are they correctly coordinating their preparations for the pas they are performing?
3. How technically pure is their performance?
4. Is the quality of their dynamics adequate, and does their phrasing set them apart from the rest?
5. How legible and how convincing is their dramatic interpretation? (Ultimately, in a good company the dancers should be at a standard where it is not so much their technique as their dramatic and musical interpretation and their expressiveness which determine their inimitability).
6. Do they have an adequate awareness of the laws which govern the stage?

And so on, and so forth. And my own exam, on which I must judge myself, is their evening's performance.

Now, working as a freelance guest teacher I have the opportunity to keep an eye on current events on the stage; in addition I am helped and taught by the blessing of our times – the video. Being able to watch great performers, productions and classes from all corners of the globe, slowing down the dancing of great technical experts so as to observe and understand their secrets – that is my daily lesson, the source of my inspiration.

The profession of a ballet master is understood variously, depending on country and language. For some it means a person who teaches a defined choreography. Meanwhile, that sort of work is more and more often done by 'choreologists', annotating the choreography on a musical stave, mainly by the Benesh method. That is not my profession.

What I am is defined in English by the word 'coach' – in Stanislavsky's dictionary, 'a stagecoach driver'. It's a fine comparison – dancers are like beautiful, noble, often exuberant, but always very sensitive steeds. It's the coachman's job to help them reach their goal safely, quickly and effectively. I aim to teach my dancers how to release their own artistic inspiration. I try to prepare them for performance in such a way that through concentration they can recreate in themselves a state of creative ecstasy, while at the same time preserving sobriety in the other half of their brains, which controls the mechanical side of the performance, so that they dance with a burning heart, but a cool head.

Woytek Lowski
Summer 1995

Gelsey Kirkland in *Romeo and Juliet*   PHOTO: LESLIE E SPATT

1

Selected exercises at the barre

To get the dancers into a mood of concentration, start the lesson with some simple exercises facing the barre executing simple battement tendus and demi-pliés from 1st position.

Pliés

Begin the exercise in 2nd position, as it is easiest for pupils who do not yet have a perfectly developed or natural turn-out. After the pliés, always bend the torso, usually starting forwards, with the feet parallel. In the plié, stress a conscious relaxation of the knees (while maintaining a correctly turned-out position). In this exercise the thighs should be flat at the front, and pulled up behind, with the inside thighs rotated forwards and with the feeling of length in the front of the groin. The distance between the knees and the pelvis does not diminish as one descends in the plié. During the descent, the spine should appear as if on a winch, in opposition to the downward direction of the movement being performed. As one rises, on the other hand, one should feel as if one is having to push oneself away from the floor with an imaginary weight on the shoulders, as if struggling against gravity. There is no pause or dead-point in the demi-plié. The knees relax in order to summon the strength to straighten out, that is, push away from the floor.

Battements tendus

In battements tendus, one must not shift the weight of the body forwards onto the toes of the working foot. The working foot extends, as if setting off on a moving pavement, but with no change in the position of the hips. One should not lean on it, or curl one's toes, thinking that this will help one to make the line of the instep look beautiful. These exercises should be done in at least three combinations, gradually increasing the tempo:

(1) From 1st position, I suggest battements tendus at a slow tempo, so that the pupil can feel the rotation of the thigh bone at the hip joint, directed downwards to the foot.
(2) Repeat at not too fast a tempo from 5th position. These can be combined with a demi-plié, and finally with a temps lié as the first conscious shift of the body weight from one leg to the other.
(3) Battements tendus from 1st and 5th positions – these should be performed at a brisk tempo, with the accent in. In 5th position it is most important that both thighs, and not just the feet should be turned out, and the weight must be equally distributed to the outer and inner edges of the feet. It should be possible to put a piece of paper under the heels, since the weight of the body rests mainly on the ball of the foot (under the toes).

Battements jetés

I also recommend two to three exercises at an increasing tempo, starting with a fluent one from 1st position through to a very fast one from 5th position. At a fast tempo, the foot does most of the work (not the thigh) since the height of the leg is lower.

Ronds de jambe à terre

Personally, I prefer to combine ronds de jambe à terre with slow grands ronds de jambe en l'air at 45 degrees from front to back and vice versa, with a flexed foot (reserving grands rond de jambe jetés until grand battements at the end of the barre).

Alternatively, with stretched foot: fondu attitude devant, straighten supporting leg carrying leg to attitude in 2nd, fondu carrying leg to attitude derrière, stretch both legs to arabesque, close. In all these cases the hip joint is gradually, slowly and deeply stimulated.

Pay vital attention to ensuring that the pelvis is motionless, the working

10

leg isolated from the hip, and the thigh and the knee of the supporting leg actively turned out (en dehors) in the opposite direction to the working leg.

Battements fondus

Pay particular attention to ensuring that the kneecap of the supporting leg is kept directly above the second and third toe, and that in demi-plié the pelvis does not change position. In performing fondus to the back, the pelvis must lean forwards to some degree, but should always remain directly above the foot of the supporting leg. In rising up on demi-pointe, the weight of the body should rest on the second and third toes.

A helpful exercise is to bend the extended working leg into attitude position with a simultaneous demi-plié of the supporting leg. Next, both knees should be straightened without the slightest loss of turn-out.

A harder version of this exercise is to perform it on demi-pointe, keeping the height of the heel unchanged during the demi-plié and straightening of the leg. This helps to develop a high strong demi-pointe especially for pirouettes. (N.B. Teachers must ensure that this strenuous exercise is performed only occasionally, and that dancers relieve the stress on the knee-joints by supporting the torso well.)

Battements frappés

In frappés with the standing foot on the floor, the foot of the working leg moves forwards with slightly relaxed toes, in order to brush the floor with the ball of the foot, and immediately extends the toes very energetically.

In men's classes one can combine the frappés simples or doubles at 45 degrees with a preparation for the cabriole, that is, with a very swift double strike with the thigh of the working leg and with the working foot flexed (the rhythm of a double cabriole), immediately throwing it outwards with the foot already extended. Both inside thigh muscles should be used strongly in this exercise.

Ronds de jambe en l'air

One should adopt the principle whereby the toes of the working

11

leg making the circling action are brought quickly in towards the supporting leg and open more slowly with resistance. The ellipse should always be performed forward of the working leg, in both ronds en dehors and en dedans. The knee and the thigh stay still.

Doubles frappés

This exercise can be combined with battements piqués, pas de cheval and fast doubles ronds de jambe en l'air at 45 degrees.

Adagio

In performing a battement développé one should raise the leg through retiré to the highest attitude position and complete the movement with the lower part of the leg without changing the position of the knee. To develop the opening further, from the en l'air position one can bend and straighten the working leg several times whilst raising the knee and maintaining a strong rotation in the hip joint. In order to strengthen students I would repeat this movement more times than I would for professional dancers with a long day of rehearsing or performing ahead of them. One can finish the adagio by bending the torso in all directions, in order to release the stress and fatigue which builds up in the lumbar region of the spine.

Petits battements

This is a swift opening of the leg to the side (like an incomplete ballonné) to a distance of several centimetres away from the supporting leg. In a basic cou-de-pied position the working foot curves around the supporting ankle, while at the same time remaining completely stretched. Finish petits battements with balancing in a major position, such as an attitude effacée or croisée.

Grands battements

The leg is raised and supported by the back of the thigh. Battements with a flexed foot deeply stimulate the hip joint by rotating the leg further in this position than is possible with the foot stretched. One can combine grands battements simples with grands battements with a flexed foot and, as previously mentioned, with grand ronds de jambe jetés. All grands battements start as battements tendus – that is, one does not precede throwing the leg outwards by deflecting and shifting the hips and torso, nor does one lean towards the working leg. In grands battements, the trunk of the body is firmly held on the supporting leg side, and is not leaning towards the barre.

General comments

In performing these exercises, it is important to keep an independent mental motor going in four areas of the body:

(1) Head–neck
(2) Shoulders–ribcage
(3) Ribcage–pelvic girdle
(4) Pelvic girdle–thighs

By ironing out excessive tension in the neck and shoulder muscles and by correctly positioning the hips and torso, one can effectively reduce effort and prevent injury. The arms are raised without raising the shoulders, and the head is turned on a relaxed neck. One should hold the barre so that it can be pushed downwards with the flat of the hand. The thumb lies on the barre. Grasping the barre and 'ripping it out of the wall' has never improved anybody's legwork.

When breathing, the torso should be expanded in a V-shape from the centre of the body, broadening the back sideways rather than pushing the ribs forward.

Remember to pull the stomach muscles tightly towards the lower part of the spine and to turn the backs of the thighs firmly forwards, whilst raising them upwards. In this way, the dancer keeps the pelvis still and can control the balance by being conscious of the body's own centre of gravity, located above its base – the whole foot, or demi-pointe. One should stand as if on top of the thigh bones. Tired dancers stimulate the body by bending the torso (port de bras) after battements tendus, ronds de jambe à terre, adagio, etc. As one bends the spine, after extending the waist upwards, one should first bend the upper part of it just above the 'corset' (corset means the muscles around the waist, which form a strong girdle) and lean in all directions without shifting the hips. When performing pirouettes, the muscles of the corset make certain undesirable twists impossible, and the body can turn as one complete whole in a vertical line.

In exercises which rely on demanding footwork, such as battements jetés, battements fondus, ronds de jambe en l'air, and so on, extend the movement in the final phase, 'with resistance' rather than 'flapping' the foot as if shaking sand from one's slippers.

It is infinitely important to use the floor for assistance and opposition, by pushing it away with the ball of the foot. One should stick one's foot to the floor as if it were a magnet, or a surface covered in glue.

Stretching at the barre may be introduced after ronds de jambe à terre or ronds de jambe en l'air or at the end of the barre after grands battements. I personally take care not to give two barre exercises in succession for the same group of muscles; that is, I split up strenuous exercises with the leg at the height of the hips (fondus, ronds de jambe en l'air, adagio, grands battements) and exercises for the foot with the leg at 45 degrees. It is a good idea to perform most of the exercises twice – first at a slow, and then at a fast tempo.

Woytek Lowski in *The Gypsy*.

Woytek Lowski as Tybalt in *Romeo and Juliet*.

2

Selected exercises in the centre

Centre practice

When I have watched experienced dancers warming up before a performance, I have noticed that their first exercises without using the barre are always very simple ones, such as uncomplicated battements tendus, temps-liés, relevés, etc. Starting exercises in the centre with very difficult strenuous elements, (such as pirouettes in major positions with a grand plié) does not have the desired effect. As a rule, dancers hop while performing these exercises, which has a negative effect on the exercises they do afterwards – that is to say, they lose their confidence from that moment on. It is in performing exercises like temps liés that the dancer should consciously, gracefully and effortlessly shift the centre of gravity from one leg to the other. Once the dancer is standing comfortably on a turned-out leg, with the entire foot glued to the floor as if by suction, conscious of the relationship between mid-pelvis and supporting foot, then the shift is easily made. In the temps lié there is no passage through any unfamiliar positions; the weight of the body rests on one leg, then it is equally distributed on both legs, and finally it moves to one leg again. One should be able to sense the floor beneath one's foot and the vertical line passing from the centre of the head, through the centre of the pelvis down to the ball of the supporting foot. If a dancer has properly completed a simple, uncomplicated but comprehensive barre without an excessive number of épaulements and turns, there should not be many problems with balance when doing exercises in the centre. In the centre, however, all exercises are performed with épaulement and fluent port de bras incorporating free use of the torso.

After battements tendus should come a short adagio in order to help feel

17

the transference of weight according to the laws of balance in the big poses. Change the raised leg, to avoid exhausting the pupil by performing a lot of développés with the same leg (this applies to men in particular). Continually pay attention to the turn-out of the supporting leg and the entire sole of the foot, which should stay glued to the floor. If both legs share the effort equally in maintaining turn-out, the pelvis (the body's centre of gravity) is immobilised, and the pupil can be made aware of controlling balance. Of course, turn-out is maintained by the inside thigh muscles and those of the backs of the legs being pulled up, inwards and forwards – not the outer part of the thighs. 'Turn-out is not what you have, but what you do with it'.

In an adagio I make a moderate use of pirouettes, in order to prepare pupils for them and to be able to develop them in the exercises that follow, combined with battements jetés, battements frappés, ronds de jambe à terre, and so on.

Sample exercises

(1) Two battements jetés à la seconde changé opening right leg, and simultaneously making a quarter-turn en dehors on the first battement. Repeat en dedans with left leg; continue en dehors with right leg, then en dedans with left leg to finish facing front again. Relevé in 5th, retiré from 5th to 4th position and pirouettes en dehors. This can be repeated in 'reverse' with pirouettes en dedans or another combination can be set in which the first part of the heel of the supporting foot (as in a pirouette en dedans) moves forwards. Grade the difficulty and complexity of combinations.

Combine a fondu with preparation for pirouettes in major positions. If the purpose of the class is to practise pirouettes in attitude, first introduce a promenade in this position. Through this, the pupil can feel how the pirouette should be performed, as the promenade is a series of mini-relevés, during which the weight of the body rests on the front of the foot. Free of weight, the heel initiates the movement. Remember that the supporting leg maintains the same turn-out at the end as at the beginning of a pirouette. If the weight of the body rests mainly on the heel and the action of the supporting leg is retarded, the torso leans forwards, the pelvis shifts backwards and the groin closes up, resulting in a loss of balance.

(2) Fondu à la seconde; with the same leg fondu croisé forwards, demi-plié transition to attitude croisée, full promenade en dedans, relevé, tombé croisé to 4th, circular port de bras in 4th position lunge as preparation, pirouette attitude en dedans, pas de bourrée. In the pirouette, as in the promenade, we keep the torso as a single compact whole, finishing the turn in the same position as we started in. Only the neck is relaxed, and the eyes return to the same point with every turn. An exception may be pirouettes in first arabesque en dedans and third arabesque en dehors, where the eyes remain motionless, directed above the fingers of the front arm.

(3) For a pirouette en dedans à la seconde to the right: perform a battement fondu croisé devant with the right leg, tombé en avant into 4th croisé, battement left leg to à la seconde (aiming for 90 degrees, but *with level hips*) en fondu en face. Next, retiré with the left leg, right leg to relevé, place left leg behind 4th croisé in preparation, pirouettes à la seconde en dedans finishing in a demi-plié with the left leg à la seconde and a pirouette en dedans in retiré position.

   The rotation from 4th to 2nd position must happen inside the pelvis, and the torso should not lean away from the leg, but should remain vertical. The pupil should understand the mechanics of the preparation, because a well-executed pirouette relies on a properly executed preparation.

   To loosen up after a difficult, strenuous fondu, do a combination with a wide shift, combining such elements as grands battements, balancés, tombés, pas de bourrée, and so on, with various pirouettes in both minor and major positions.

   The musical accompaniment could be an expansive waltz, or better, a mazurka. The combination should be as varied in its choreography as possible, with full involvement of the torso and épaulement, and the hands can give the character of, for example, a Polish, Hungarian, Russian or Spanish dance.

Allegro

At the start of petit allegro, small jumps from both legs to both legs are obligatory, since taking off or landing on one leg as the first jump of the day is inadvisable and potentially harmful. Thus one might recommend changements de pieds, échappés in 1st, 2nd, 4th and 5th positions, and so on. A tough and difficult but useful exercise is a sauté taking off from the toes alone, in order to strengthen them without demi-plié. Always be careful to soften the landing to the heels through the use of demi-pointe. In Balanchine's technique, changements are a minimal opening of the legs, in order to cross them as quickly as possible in 5th position in the air before landing. It is the same in pas assemblé, where the take-off leg joins the leg thrown upwards, to close in 5th during the upward jump. The dancer should land in a well-crossed 5th position. This requires great strength and speed in the action of the jumping leg. Perform assemblés at a medium tempo using the muscles of the entire thighs. Do not make the accompaniment too fast – the most important thing is a slightly deeper demi-plié. Descending from the jump, return first on the toes, and gradually, moving through demi-pointe set the heels down. After the above exercises, the tempo of the class should increase. Now introduce jetés, ballonnés, ballottés, batterie, etc.

There are two ways of performing a jeté. The first is by keeping 2nd position in the air with the knees straight, landing in a cou-de-pied position once the floor is reached. In the second, as in Balanchine, the jumping leg reaches the cou-de-pied position during the jump while in the air, and is held there to land in this position afterwards. If the purpose of assemblés is to land gently through demi-pointe on to the ball of the foot, then the purpose of jetés, temps levés and batteries is to pick up speed and take off upwards like a ping-pong ball, to strengthen the toes and develop their speed of reaction. At an increasing tempo it works the feet and toes even faster. In his choreography Balanchine often demands such a speedy tempo that there is no time to set the heels down. In jetés and temps levés, the knee of the take-off leg bends very little. In this case, great strength and speed of the toes and metatarsus are important. The bend of the leg on which the dancer returns after the jump reduces as the speed increases. Men in particular should combine jetés with batterie, repeating each exercise over and over, at increasing speed but with no loss of precision. For students, the tempo for jetés can be slower, and care should be taken over how the heels are placed after the jump. The dancer should achieve lightness, giving the impression that the floor is pushing him off, not dragging him down.

Next introduce medium jumps such as various types of sissonnes. Here, precise execution of the demi-plié and mastery of space are all-important. By contrast with petit allegro, medium jumps pay particular attention to a deep, fluent return to the demi-plié, maintaining the set position which is a crucial preparation for grand allegro. This is mainly relevant to certain kinds of sissonnes, pas failli, temps levés in major positions, entrechats six and grands assemblés de volée, and so on.

Only after these exercises should one introduce large jumps, or grand allegro. There are new elements in the men's grand allegro which have become familiar relatively recently: big jumps with double turns in major positions, or with a change of position between the first and second turn. Since the sensation of turning in a horizontal position is entirely different from the vertical position, the preparation for learning it will be a single rivoltade.

Finish the lesson with a coda: for the boys a combination with tours en l'air or grandes pirouettes, and for the girls fouettés or fast turns on the diagonal. For everybody, as a final exercise, set an enchaînement en manège – essential in developing a swift unconstrained turn of the head.

'Linking steps'

In choreography, many steps are introduced which have a different form from their school form, because of tempo. Among these are exercises combining, for example, the pas de bourrée and the glissade.

Balanchine's pas de bourrée is performed with straight knees, there is no sur le cou-de-pied in the transfer from leg to leg, and the step is performed on 'one'. There is almost no 2nd position in the legs, and only 1st position in the transfer; immediately after that the legs are crossed into 5th position. This pas finishes on demi-pointe in 5th position, and the demi-pointe of one leg is placed directly in front of the toes of the other. Thus the lower limbs cross

21

over so firmly that only the front leg is visible.

Another step which has changed is the glissade. It also is performed on 'one', without shifting the body weight from one leg to the other. All that remains is the maximum straightening of the toes just above the floor. In the middle phase of the pas, the body weight is located exactly between the two legs. The glissade is like a small pair of scissors, opened to the distance of one foot and no more. The toes of both feet are simultaneously in 2nd or 4th position just above the floor. The 'one' is the close to 5th position with both legs simultaneously. This helps to speed up the tempo of the petit allegro. At a fast tempo there is no time for more. The same principles apply with a glissade to the side, front or back. Great care should be taken over the neatness of preparations for jumps. Preparations such as the pas couru, pas de bourrée and glissade must be performed with maximum turn-out and extension, and the final take-off before the jump cannot be done from the heel with the thighs positioned en dedans. The leap should come from a turned-out take-off leg, the last thing to tear itself away from the floor. Placing the foot en dedans spoils the line of the entire jump; dancers often only take trouble over the start of their preparation, performing their take-off into the jump inaccurately, without being conscious of the correct line of the whole body.

Arms

In all classical exercises, the arms and hands fulfil an essential function, in terms of both technique and expression. Their actions should be as well co-ordinated as possible with the action of the head, legs and trunk. The co-ordination and function of the hands is particularly significant when performing jumps. At the moment of take-off, the preparation should look as if the hands are 'taking' the leg with them, and passing through 1st position to fling it upwards. With time, 1st position of the hands loses its set line and the hands work freely; it is important, however, for them to help to shift the centre of gravity above the foot of the jumping leg. This movement must take place so quickly as to be almost invisible. This is essential to the achievement of lightness and co-ordination in the jump. The hands should aim downwards when the whole body is tending downwards; when the leg is aiming upwards, the hands should be helping it at the same tempo, as wings help birds. There is a relaxation before the jump, but just before the motion upwards at the moment of take-off there is a tensing of all the muscles, most of all those of the take-off leg, and then an immediate relaxation in the air.

Watching a cat leap, we can see an enormous concentration of energy before the jump. This energy will be released at the moment of take-off, then comes the phase of flight and landing. The technique of a jump relies on proper use of the strength of all the muscles with perfect coordination of movement. The height of the jump depends to a large extent on the speed of the initial ascent, and thus, among other things, on one's ability to amass a great amount of energy and then release it at the moment of take-off.

Pirouettes

As an important principle for correctly performing a pirouette, one should adopt the position from which the pirouettes are to be performed quickly, and as correctly as possible. In performing a pirouette from 4th for example, remember that the hips should be level in the demi-plié, and that this position should be maintained in the relevé. In the preparation, the weight of the body should rest mostly on the front leg. The supporting leg on which the turn is made should be turned out to the maximum extent during the relevé – pushed above the second and third toes. In the course of the relevé, the impression should be given that the weight of the body is resting 'on top' of the thigh bone, and the hip should be over the foot of the supporting leg.

In performing a pirouette from 4th, Balanchine recommends a very firm crossing of the legs in the preparation, so that the demi-pointe of the leg on which the pirouette is performed is directly beneath the centre of the pelvis. The demi-plié before the pirouette, both en dehors and en dedans, is performed by the knee of the front leg alone; the back knee remains straight.

In performing a pirouette, the main driving force – the motor for the turn – is the legs, not the arms. In a pirouette to the right, the left side initiates the turn by 'chasing' the right knee, which is kept firmly turned-out to the side in retiré position. If the left side stops while turning to the right, for

23

example, opposition is created which greatly hinders the turn.

In a pirouette en dedans, the movement is initiated by the supporting leg. Take as an example a tour in attitude effacée en dedans. First go into relevé, and fractionally afterwards (without stopping of course) comes the turn. The waist muscles help to maintain the position in a single, complete figure. Often the chief error is that the upper part of the body turns faster than the lower, or vice versa. In performing pirouettes en dedans, teachers usually demand that immediately after the preparation the working leg adopts the retiré position front. A pirouette en dedans with degagé is a completely different sort of turn. It is like a fouetté en dedans – the leg and arms are opened to the side, and then brought together simultaneously, while the arms close, from the elbows, to 1st position.

In performing turns do not tense the outer neck muscles. The neck should be supported by the inner muscles of the central area. It should be loose and as fully extended as possible. In a pirouette, it is essential to turn the head rhythmically and to position it by turning it as far as possible towards the audience. Also important in pirouettes are proper actions of the hands, which should be relaxed. 1st and 2nd positions of the arms should not be too high.

In Balanchine's technique, when turning en dehors to the right, the right arm gathers force by aiming the hand at the left shoulder and extending forwards (it does not open to 2nd position). At this moment, the left arm should remain completely still. During the turn, both arms cross, and if the pirouettes are performed to the right, the left forearm crosses on the outside of the right. Another method is to open the arms to 2nd position, bringing them together to a shortened, low 1st position during the turn. It is simply a matter of style. In completing pirouettes or tours, the body should remain on its axis, and the turn should finish in the same position in which it began. Do not hop either during or after the turn. The lumbar and stomach muscles should be kept firmly tensed during a pirouette. Do not relax the knee of the leg on which one is turning. Come down from a pirouette with a so-called 'pulled-up' knee. During the turn, slowly exhale in order to contract the lower part of the ribs, rather than the frequent but mistaken practise of inhaling. In fact, inhaling in the course of a turn causes the dancer to lean backwards and lose balance.

In a pirouette, the distance between the hips and the ribs must be identical on both sides; the raised leg should not fall either during the turn or in the demi-plié, and the side of the working leg should not twist. The pelvis should not move; it is as if it is full of water which must not be spilled. One may aptly compare pirouettes with a spiral or a revolving door, which turns on a vertical axis. The weight of the body should remain on the demi-pointe of the supporting leg to the very end and should not be shifted. Some ballerinas finish their pirouettes on demi-pointe or pointe, which is very beautiful. However, one should not draw out the end of the exercise, and if the boys perform a greater number of turns, one should adapt the rhythm of the entire exercise to that. A ballerina was once filmed performing a fouetté. In six of the frames, one could see her eyes, and only two frames captured her from behind. This means that she was working with a relaxed, long neck. In performing pirouettes, the dancer should imagine he is being filmed, and should execute his turns to avoid being shot either from the back or the side, only the front. The accent should always be kept to the front. Pirouettes are not just a matter of 'whirling round' at an even tempo. In pirouettes which are to finish in a major position, it is essential to maintain a correct, turned out position all the way through, and to lower oneself from the relevé through the heels, only opening the working leg in the freely chosen direction afterwards. In the retiré position, the hips remain level, with only the knee raised as high as possible; only at the moment when one extends one's leg higher can one raise the hip slightly. This is the golden rule when performing a battement développé in an adagio, and for example when adopting a major position after pirouettes. However, if the aim is a pirouette à la seconde, one must not change the position of the hips, because neither a balance nor a pirouette can be achieved in that way. For men in grandes pirouettes à la seconde it is important to finish each of them facing the audience. One must not relax the turn-out of either leg. The left arm (turning to the right) remains in 2nd position in front of the torso and should always remain in the dancer's field of view. In terms of musicality, the approach to the position and the first turn is performed on 'and', and completed on 'one'.

In teaching pirouettes, accompaniment is vitally important. The accompaniment should be chosen to suit the character of the pirouette and the speed at which it is being performed; the turns of the body should correspond to the music. If it is an allegro tempo, the pirouettes are faster, and if the music is slow, the turns are slower too, which creates the impression that we are dancing pirouettes, not just doing them. Pirouettes cannot be separated from a dance, they should have their own expression and character.

Exercises on pointe

Teachers should plan the barre preceding a class on pointe with the aim of warming up and strengthening the muscles and tendons of the feet. In the course of such a barre, one should pay particular attention to strengthening the muscles around the ankles and the sole of the foot. In exercises at the barre preceding a class on pointe, one gets the best results from a great number of battements tendus, battements jetés and pas de cheval. After these exercises, pointe shoes are put on and work can begin on well-stimulated feet.

Sample exercises

(1) The first exercise is performed facing the barre, the next sideways to it, using it as an aid but without gripping it tightly. In 1st position, demi-plié and relevé (on 'one' and 'two'). Set the heels on the floor without a demi-plié (on 'one' and 'two') push away from the floor and go into a relevé with firmly pulled up knees (on 'one' and 'two'). Do the same in 2nd position. During this exercise one should pull down the muscles located just below the buttocks, in order to maintain even turn-out in both legs. However, this doesn't mean tensing the buttocks, just firmly drawing the inside thigh muscles together.

Next the same exercise is done on one leg, with the other leg in a sur le cou-de-pied back position. Facing the barre, the dancers relevé on one leg – through the centre of the foot, the entire leg remaining straight. This is another instance when one should not allow oneself to grasp hold of the barre, but just to use it as an aid, gently pushing down on it and locking the shoulder-blades down.

Perform the same exercise with the leg in attitude, remembering to keep the raised leg held at a perfect right angle, with the shoulders level in relation to the hips, then with the leg à la seconde, with the leg raised to 90 degrees or 45 degrees. The same may be done with the leg raised en avant and en arrière. To come down from pointe, one should use the strength of the foot muscles. One should not allow oneself to fall off pointe, but should descend gradually, using all the foot muscles on the way. When lowering the heels the weight of the body should remain on the front part of the foot for as long as possible.

Slowly coming down off pointe, the foot should feel as if it is squashing something.

(2) The next exercise is a fondu on pointe. Take 5th position relevé, then fondu forwards with the right leg, fondu back with the left leg, fondu à la seconde, passé and balance. The arms help one to keep one's balance by passing from the preparatory position through 1st to 3rd. This exercise is a useful preparation for hops on pointe.

In a perfectly pulled-up body, nothing changes; there is no lean away from the working leg.

(3) Next, also at the barre, perform an adagio on pointe. Battement développé front, bending the leg into attitude, port de bras forward and back, and test the balance. This exercise should be performed first with one leg, then the other.

(4) The next exercise at the barre may be shifting from leg to leg in major positions, slowly coming off pointe onto demi-pointe and then to the heel. Piqué to arabesque, demi-plié in this position, piqué onto the back leg with the front one at 90 degrees and so on. In the arabesque, the pelvis remains over the foot, the torso leans forwards. One inclines the upper torso, not just the waist. Do not contract, but elongate the lumbar region.

Now move into the centre, and perform an adagio in pointe shoes, standing on the entire foot, so that one can feel the toes well, arranging one's feet in the shoes to avoid wobbling and uncertainty. It would be advisable to perform the exercise with an arabesque penchée. Next introduce a combination of exercises from two legs onto two legs, relevé on one leg, piqué on one leg, relevé in major positions, piqué in major positions, turns. In this way we can prepare the students for harder tasks while they are still becoming aware of their degree of difficulty.

Sample exercises

Demi-plié in 5th position, retiré relevé with the right leg front, demi-plié in 5th position, retiré relevé with left leg back, demi-plié in 5th, passé and 4th position back, (preparation for pirouette) with the right leg, relevé from 4th position to retiré front, close 5th. Later repeat this with one or more turns instead of the retiré. In performing the relevé, the foot of the supporting leg should be under the centre of the pelvis, while the toes of the other leg follow the line of the tibia of the supporting leg in adopting the retiré position.

To perform one pirouette, do the same retiré and maintain the same balance as in the preceding exercise without turning, but this time add a turn of the head. The arms should not help too much here; they should not make any movements, nor should they bend. Emphasise the fact that the force for the pirouette comes from the feet (pushing away from the floor and attaining the desired position as quickly as possible). This means that in the turn the body is vertical, on an axis where one loses one's sense of weight – as if the force of gravity did not exist. For one pirouette, no force with the arms is necessary. In a single pirouette, only the feet and the head do the work, they alone give the impetus for the turn.

If the beginning and end of the pirouette is kept in the same position, it will be nothing more than just a demi-plié, relevé retiré, but with a turn. The same exercise can be done with a double turn.

For a greater number of pirouettes, perform a slightly deeper demi-plié and push away the floor forcefully: little movements of the head are enough to make additional turns – that is, the pirouettes move in a spiral upwards, not along an ellipse.

Very often the arms, instead of helping in a turn, obstruct and hamper one from maintaining the vertical. Instead, they should support the torso in a position which cannot alter during the turns. To put it another way, the arms help one to keep the whole body, with the exception of the head and neck, in a solid figure during the turn.

Next do turns with a shift through a piqué to the right or left. The torso shifts as a whole in one solid figure, in harmony with the principles of balance. Doing a turn into a piqué we shift as if the coccyx is above the toes of the supporting leg. In the piqué, one must place the foot perfectly along the line in which one is moving. The hips shift in the same way. Musically speaking, on 'one' the head, on a loose neck, is already turned forwards after the first pirouette.

Here it is important to push away from the floor. The force in these turns is directed into the depths of the floor (resistance to the force of gravity). The number of pirouettes can be increased with corresponding actions of the head. Dancers who perform multiple turns do not make more movements of the arms, but increase the number of turns through whipping the head and lightly pushing back the knee in the passé position. The more forcefully one pushes back the knee, the more powerfully one should raise the stomach muscles upwards, in order to block the pelvis.

General comments

In the teaching of classical dance it is vital for the pupils to master the skill of breathing. Above all, one's breathing should be in harmony with the music. When it is, one creates the impression that the dance, as perceived by the audience, is being performed effortlessly – the movements are light, flowing from one to the next in a natural way. In classical dance one breathes mainly with the upper part of the chest.

One should lower one's hands at the same time as exhaling, moving one's fingers as if pushing the air downwards. Preparation of the hands should be in harmony with the dancer's natural breathing, and the 'breathing' in the music. Hand movements begin from the diaphragm, through the shoulders, arm, wrist and fingers.

During the dance one should listen to the music and internally sing an accompaniment. The impulse for the movement of the arms is rooted in the back – shoulder-blade – (where the 'wings' grow) travelling through a well-supported upper arm and elbow. It then continues along the forearm to the hands, which should sensitively complete the phrase of the music. If the dance does not give the spectator an aesthetic impression, it means that the dancers are not dancing with the torso, they are not dancing with the whole body – they are just performing individual steps in a completely thoughtless or mechanical way. It is essential for the dancer to be fully conscious of the correct performance of his movements and to have the skill to correct them. He should 'keep a mirror in his brain, on the screen of his imagination'.

To be full and expansive, a movement should use the forces of opposition: in turning to the right, for example, the movement begins from the left; movement downwards is preceded by movement upwards; movement upwards by movement downwards.

In Balanchine, since the dancers dance at a fast tempo, and stages have hard floors, big jumps all but disappear into the choreography. They become very flat, because one has to cover the whole stage with them. A long stop in demi-plié after a jump does not exist at all – it is impossible, even for men. However, in a traditional ballet such as *Giselle*, a deep demi-plié after a jump is necessary to get the maximum height in the allegro. This is what Natalia Makarova had in mind when speaking of differences in dance styles: 'All dancers speak the same language, but with different accents'. Since a repertoire consists of various types of choreography and many different styles, today's dancers must be able to 'speak with many accents', they must have broad mental horizons. One should therefore acquaint students with all kinds of techniques and a diversity of dance styles. Yet to understand how these particular styles vary from another, one has to learn from the very best sources, the very best specialists. In most cases, style is a question of musicality and use of the arms. One knows that one's legs must be turned out and must maintain the en dehors position and an extended instep, that one should stay vertical and on balance. Style is musicality, épaulement and port de bras; arm movements – port de bras – should also be linked with the way one uses the shoulders. One should build up such strength, and above all suppleness in the upper back, so that this carries the hands into space; then the movement looks lively and natural.

A good illustration of the question of musicality is given by the dancers of New York City Ballet – trained by the school of American Ballet and Balanchine's repertoire. The difference between them and any other trained dancer is immediately apparent in class. With Balanchine, all preparations occur before the beat. On the strong accent, the dancer is in the air in the desired position. The high point of the movement, such as a jump or battement, is combined with a strong accent; at the top of a step, a position is held, as if recorded on a photograph. The difference is that while others are just beginning their jump, Balanchine's dancers are already in the air.

Returning to the plié, I would stress once again that one should be aware of its various forms. There is the soft, deep plié, as required in romantic traditional ballets. In Balanchine, the plié is practically invisible, since the feet are so strong that they take on a significant amount of the work of the knees, and particularly of the thighs. There is no sitting in the plié, it is simply the fastest possible straightening of the knees from a minimal demi-plié, which demands great strength in the lower part of the legs. The main feature of the choreography of Balanchine, of his many imitators and those who have gained and continue to gain inspiration from his genius, is his inexhaustible dynamic energy. It reminds one of everyday life in New York, which is more like racing than walking down the street. Here you must fight to survive. If you don't hurry and engage all the energy you can muster at any given moment, you perish. This phenomenon is reflected in dance. Even women's dancing loses certain nuances and sophisticated elegance; sometimes it is more like a sporting discipline. Here the essence of dance is covering space quickly, fast footwork and fluent leg movements. Thus it is a unique language which differs from that of European countries.

In Eastern Europe, greater emphasis is placed on what happens above the waist; in the West the stress is on leg and footwork. If one could use various languages of dance simultaneously, one would have ideal dancing.

For the ideal classroom, one would need Russian arms, British or French placement of the body and American feet. However, every classical ballet technique has a characteristic style; for example, in Bournonville port de bras the forearm passes from up to down in the same position, with charming simplicity; its placement does not change. This is a stylistic idiosyncrasy which would be out of place in the imperial splendours of Petipa, and finds its exact opposite in the jazzy, broken undulations of Balanchine. Yet each has its own beauty within the proper context, and must be respected.

Similarly, one cannot, for example, compare ballerinas from the East with those of the West, Maya Plisetskaya, for example, with Margot Fonteyn, or Gelsey Kirkland. The fact is that although at the same artistic level, great artistes from different countries are very different from one another. Numerous factors play a role in forming public taste in different countries: education, historical development, literature, tradition and so on. American taste is very different from Russian or French, so a dancer who is regarded as an idol in one country may have no appeal in another.

Maya Plisetskaya in *The Fountain of Bakhchisaray.*

Gelsey Kirkland and Anthony Dowell in *Romeo and Juliet*.   PHOTO: LESLIE E SPATT

3

General comments on classes

Purpose and length of classes

It is important for each lesson to be planned in detail and to have a specific purpose. If, for example, the purpose is to work on grands fouettés, then include some elements of this in the first exercises at the barre, leading on to them through battements fondus, grands battements, and further on through exercises in the centre, small, medium and grand allegro.

In classical dance teaching it is vital to master technique and build up the dancers' strength. One of the ways in which one gains strength is by repeating simple, uncomplicated exercises. This may be formulated in the following rule: strength is built up through repetition, not complication. One should also be aware that exercises should be combined in such a way that the dancer can always feel his own centre of gravity. This too should be a golden rule. Rosella Hightower in her exercises puts great emphasis on the action of the supporting leg, claiming that if one is standing correctly on that leg, it is quite simply impossible to exercise badly. It is so determinative that it forces the other leg to work correctly. Exercises at the barre for students should last 40–45 minutes. In the theatre, a whole class might consist of the following: 30–40 minutes of barre, 30 minutes of exercises in the centre, 20–30 minutes of jumps. The difference between the Soviet and Western system of class is that under the Soviet system, after twice repeating each exercise one goes on to the next one, while in the West the dancers repeat each exercise until they feel that they have mastered it fully.

In Western companies, the grand adagio in the centre has been virtually eliminated and replaced by more work at the barre. In the centre, from a basic and simple adagio we lead into other combinations. At the barre, a balance for example is performed after each exercise. In an adagio in the centre, one tends to change the working leg as often as possible. Instead of continually repeating a step to try and master it, it would be better to understand the mechanics of the movement. One should not introduce a lot of long and difficult combinations into the lesson. Rather, it is important for the lesson to be simple, so that the dancers have time to perfect a step instead of thinking about choreography. A grand allegro can be contained within 16 bars, and then it is not too tiring, but one may repeat it several times in order to perfect its performance. In schools, a port de bras and bow are obligatory at the end of each lesson, while in companies of mature dancers, the tempo of the lesson reaches the maximum, and exercises such as the manège, grandes pirouettes, tours en l'air for the boys, and so on, are introduced. In France, at the Paris Opéra where the classes are longer, the ballerinas put on pointe shoes after medium jumps. At this point, the men do combinations of grand allegro, then the women do exercises on pointe for about 10–15 minutes. This is the constant rule at every class.

In the USA, in most cases, the ballerinas only put on pointe shoes and exercise on their own after class, or work on pointe later on during rehearsals for a show. However some teachers may require them to put on pointe shoes during daily training after the barre and get them to perform as many exercises as possible on pointe, but this relates only to very advanced professional ballerinas.

Responsibilities of the student

For a classical dancer to achieve true artistic effect, the attitude he holds towards his profession and to the company he happens to work with is as much a determining factor as his familiarity with the elements of technique. It may be set out in the following recommendations:

1. A dancer should have courtesy towards his teacher and colleagues.
2. The dancer should always aspire to master the assigned step and enchaînements as quickly as possible, respond well to the music he is dancing to (tempo, time signature, and so on).

3. The dancer must be aware of the space which he and the other dancers occupy during their work.

4. The dancer should prepare himself for each class, rehearsal, or performance. He should enter them in a mood of calm and concentration, so that in passing into the world of the discipline of classical dance he can recreate the teacher's previous suggestions and comments in his mind, overcome the pressure of nerves by strength of will, and through even, conscious breathing, gain a sense of balance and inner calm. At every moment of the class he should be ready in position before the first chord of the music. On the first 'and' he should take a breath, be aware of his balance, and start to move his arms, first raising his elbows, while at the same time firmly lowering his shoulders. At this moment he should feel physical satisfaction before the exercise which is about to begin, and should mobilise the relevant amount of energy to perform it.

Responsibilities of the teacher

1. Respect students as fellow artistes.

2. Try to remain impartial (not an easy task), dividing your attention equally in a class.

3. Both student and teacher should start each day afresh, without carrying negative feelings and insecurities from before. For example, someone missing a pirouette for several days should not block their coordination with tension by anticipating disaster before it happens and the teacher must remain open to the possibility of an imminent breakthrough.

4. Be prepared – don't waste the student's precious time (especially in the situation of an open class). There are some dancers in companies who come to class only because the management is checking if they are present. That is their problem!

5. The dancer's health is in some degree your responsibility – think carefully when preparing a class. Take into account how strenuous the dancer's previous day was (it could have been two performances or a day off) and also how strenuous the rest of his day is going to be.

6. When dancers are concentrating and working hard, a certain tension and

37

frustration may appear when the results are not wholly successful – this is where your sense of humour and support can help a great deal as you search together for the solution.

7. There is a different key to each individual, but they all need help, attention and affection to feel secure. When dancers feel secure they will have confidence.

8. Dancers need corrections – not put-downs!

9. Keep an eye open towards what is happening in the world of teaching: read, watch videos, see others teaching classes, enlarge your vocabulary, learn and improve. To pass on tradition is a great thing, but not mindlessly.

Vladimir Vasiliev in *Spartacus.*

Woytek Lowski in Maurice Béjart's *Ninth Symphony*.

4

Practical advice for the ballet artiste

1. Stand in such a way that you feel tall and light.
2. Lengthen your body through its central axis.
3. Distribute your body weight equally between the outer and inner edges of your foot, to protect yourself, for example, from bruising when returning to the floor after a jump.
4. Keep your coccyx above the centre of your foot (when positioned on one leg) or between the centre of your feet (when positioned on both legs).
5. Increase the length of the lower part of your spine by drawing the coccyx downwards (not under) and by drawing the front of your pelvis upwards.
6. Your spine (and particularly the coccyx) should always be between and above the inside thighs when you are standing on both legs, and above the inside thigh of your supporting leg when you are standing on one leg. For example, in arabesque the coccyx should be over the toes of the supporting leg. In 4th position, which is the preparation for pirouettes, while the front leg is in demi-plié and the back leg is straight, the coccyx is located over the leg on which the pirouette is performed.
7. Keep both legs identically turned out and always stay balanced. These two elements must be synchronised.
8. You must not lose turn-out when you need to adjust the position of your hips.
9. Six deep-set rotators located behind the hip joint help to maintain turn-out. These short, thick muscles are suited to prolonged effort.
10. The turn-out of the feet depends on the degree of rotation in the hip joint.

11. Any rotation of a straight leg must start from the hip joint.

12. The thigh bones, knees and second and third toes of both feet should form a single line in a turned-out position or parallel position, and should work as a single entity in any rotational movement.

13. Lack of stability in the pelvis makes it impossible to maintain turn-out, and is a sign that the girdle muscles and the lumbar-hip muscles are not working correctly.

14. Turn-out is maintained by muscle control, and is not a mechanical, un-thinking action. Turn-out is not what you have, but what you do with what you have.

15. To maintain turn-out, elongate the muscles at the back of your legs and work them forwards with the inside thigh muscles.

16. Rotation is always controlled by the upper leg (the thigh).

17. Visible stress is a sign of incorrect muscle work. Among properly trained dancers, the effort is imperceptible because they are using individual groups of muscles consciously and expertly.

18. The spine is like a chain hanging on a ring fastened beneath the skull and weighted downwards by a heavy ball (the force of gravity). Opposing forces are at work, originating in the waist.

19. Always remain conscious of the distance separating the ribs from the hips.

20. Stretch your spine upwards starting from the waist-line, and stretch your working leg as far from the hip as possible, without disturbing its placement.

21. The pelvic bone on the supporting leg side should not drop, but should remain lifted, maintaining the length of the hip tendons – one should 'stand on the top' of the thigh bone, not 'sitting' on the leg.

22. Seek a sense of balance at the centre of the crown of the head. The head should be light, giving the impression that it is rising upwards with every movement of the body.

23. Narrow the lower part of the chest by pulling it in with the muscles.

24. Lengthen the lumbar region of the spine by using the abdominal muscles.

25. Lower the shoulders and shoulder-blades to open the upper part of the chest fully.

26. By following the principles of correct placement and action of the torso, one releases pressure from the top of the chest, which allows one to breathe freely.

27. 'Squeeze' the stomach muscles into the lower region of the spine.

28. In port de bras, first 'lift' yourself up, lengthen the waist, stretch the spine upwards and only then bend.

29. Start to bend from the upper back.

30. Your hand should rest lightly on the barre – you shouldn't grasp it ('parrot's claws' are forbidden).

31. The hands, and particularly the arms, gather strength when preparing for turning and balancing, whereas staying on balance requires more strength than turning.

32. While moving into positions, the hands never cross the centre of the body. The right hand belongs to the right side, and the left hand to the left side of the torso. It is the top of the arm which leads the hands. In positions where it is necessary to cross one's wrists (for example, in *Giselle* Act II) the elbows always remain on the outside.

33. The plié is a conscious loosening of the knees while preserving turn-out. It only takes place in the knees and does not disturb the placement of the body.

34. As one lowers in plié, the head becomes a means to lengthen the spine.

35. In performing a grand plié, the back thigh muscles support the torso as one descends, and draw together as one rises.

36. The aim of a plié is not just to stretch one's muscles, but also to gather strength for take-off.

37. The depth of a plié should never effect a change in the position of the pelvis, since the rotation in the hip joint must be isolated and controlled throughout the entire movement.

38. A good plié is fluent and alive. One should never sit in a plié.

39. Lowering in plié, you should have a sense of rising, and as you lift upwards, you should feel a gravitational pull downwards, like a weight on your shoulders.

40. Many steps are preceded by a demi-plié, and start just as one comes out

of it, for example a demi-plié in fourth position before a pirouette, in which the pirouette is performed just after coming out of the plié (do not start the turn while still in plié).

41. Vary the depth of a demi-plié when it forms the appropriate link between one movement and the next; thus it is smaller for an entrechat quatre, and deeper for an entrechat six.

42. A pirouette is a balance while turning.

43. During the turn, the dancer maintains the same position while moving upwards, as in a spiral.

44. Almost every step begins and ends with a battement tendu.

45. Each extension forward of the battement tendu (performed by making use of the floor) should serve to strengthen the metatarsus and toes for take-off, and each closing of the battement tendu into position should build up strength for landing.

46. The back of the supporting leg is always perpendicular to the floor.

47. Keeping one's toes 'glued' to the floor helps to broaden the foot – the aim being to keep one's foot properly adhered to its base of support.

48. The impulse for a battement tendu is sent out from the upper part of the leg. The action of the leg is isolated in the hip joint, which excludes all movement of the pelvis.

49. During a battement tendu relevé, extend the back muscles of your legs. Just as you position your foot, your centre of gravity should be in the central axis of the body.

50. Pull up and do not relax the muscles around the knees; always stand on stretched legs.

51. In closing in each position, your weight should be evenly distributed on both feet, to rest the supporting leg.

52. Gain strength by working the supporting leg in opposition to the floor (the vectors of energy work in opposition: the supporting leg pushes off from the floor, while the working leg opens in opposition to the supporting leg).

53. When changing from one position to another with your leg en l'air, the movement begins in the hip joint of the supporting leg. When raising

the working leg avoid leaning away from it.

54. When raising your leg to higher than natural positions (which are approximately 17 degrees back, 45 degrees sideways, and 60 degrees front) and the pelvis has to adjust, the torso adjusts itself to the working leg; the upper part should create opposition to guarantee correct performance of the exercise, and should resist leaning off balance.

55. Before lowering the leg from an extension (battement relevé lent or battement développé) one should slightly raise the leg as if it 'takes a breath' before being lowered.

56. As one performs a battement relevé lent, a battement développé or a grand battement, one should feel that the strength and impetus are coming from the muscles of the inside thigh and back of the leg.

57. The pelvis is like a container with water – don't splash it around.

58. In extensions to 90 degrees, the pelvis should not alter its basic position, which is achieved by rotating within the hip of the raised leg, that is, turning out from underneath.

59. As one lifts the leg in arabesque, the spine takes on a curve, trying to maintain the same length throughout. At the same time, the abdominal muscles must firmly support the supporting leg side to reduce some of the pressure in the lumbar region.

60. Do not allow yourself to contract and lower the working side of the torso as the working leg lowers back into position.

61. As you raise your leg, lengthen your spine even more in counteraction.

62. A rond de jambe à terre is a constant even rotation of the head of the femur in its socket.

63. In rond de jambe en dedans or en dehors à terre, the movement of the working leg is led by the heel and the inside thigh.

64. In rond de jambe en l'air, the thigh stays still.

65. When the working foot passes through 1st position in a rond de jambe à terre, it must be relaxed.

66. In battements frappés, the thigh stays still.

67. Petits battements are like little ballonnés.

68. In grands battements, the inside muscles of the working leg lead it out

and support it as it is lowered.

69. Lower from demi-pointe by gradually relaxing the sole of the foot.

70. At the top of every jump, a dancer should attain a state of balance in the air.

71. As he lands from a jump, the dancer resists gravity by landing through the foot, using the metatarsus as he does when closing a battement tendu.

72. Do not relax the muscles in the small of the back in the demi-plié after a jump. Keep the shoulder-blades pulled downwards.

73. All accepted positions and movements of classical dance and the perform-ance of each step should be technically correct; at the same time, the performer should feel – and it should appear to the audience – that no demands are being made on the body.

74. One gains extra strength to perform steps by using less strength to stay on balance.

75. A dancer should never interrupt the fluency of a movement; if he does a step wrongly in class or performance, he should avoid instant self-criti-cism and neurotic frustration, he should not immediately start pulling faces. On the contrary, he should think ahead and look forward to the next step with pleasure.

76. Begin by creating a pure image of the required movement in your imagi-nation – look at it on the screen of your imagination.

77. One can impart all sorts of information to a pupil, but how well it is assimilated and understood depends on the receptiveness of the student. It is only the dance student who can complement the teacher-artiste who stands before him.

78. The secret of achieving success in the art of dance is persistent hard work, precise mastery of each step rendered sublime through sensitivity. Talent itself is nothing more than a valuable opportunity.

79. If dancing lacks spirit, it seems dry and empty. If you lack awareness of your own personal experience, how can you dance with your heart and soul?

80. A perfect performance should be like spending time in a peaceful place somewhere inside yourself.

Gelsey Kirkland in *Romeo and Juliet.*   PHOTO: LESLIE E SPATT

47

Woytek Lowski in George Balanchine's *Prodigal Son*.

5

Working in the dance world

Stage fright

Stage fright is a fear of appearing in some unusual or important situation, particularly in front of an audience, and the conviction that in spite of being well prepared, you aren't going to perform well. Stage fright paralyses your thoughts, and won't let you concentrate. It is an irrational feeling of discomfort or threat (which was absent during rehearsals), brought on by throwing yourself into the stream of performing actions. A strong emotion, stage fright is accompanied by numerous physiological symptoms; changes in the action of the heart, breathing rhythms, and sweating. It is a very difficult and multifaceted problem, and there are really no radical solutions to avoiding it. That doesn't mean, though, that being aware of exactly what stage fright is can't help one to overcome it.

The dancer's profession, relying as it does on public performances, entails situations which inevitably set off stage fright. The basic causes usually include general apprehension at performing the required tasks, an inability to perform them, and not enough conscious work on them; an intensified feeling of responsibility, a low number of previous public performances, worry at being judged by public opinion, fear of failure, excessive ambition, a bad frame of mind, lack of belief in oneself. Awareness of the causes of stage fright is very helpful in fighting it. The pupil can eliminate quite a lot of them himself, but in many cases, the teacher's help is indispensable.

Children generally have great confidence in their teachers, and their influence very often remains of lasting value. In dealing with this situation, a ballet school teacher, particularly someone who teaches in a professional school, should aim to reduce his pupil's sensitivity to negative inner reactions by training him to be flexible enough to overcome stage fright. Get the pupil accustomed to having other people present during classes; then rehearsals in front of a whole company, and finally public performances. Each of these experiences is a stage on the 'stairway' of the dancer's life, the stairway towards self-perfection. A performance should be treated as just another 'step on the stairway'.

Of course, performance on stage is a major experience, and any hesitation, any shadow of uncertainty before performing a technically difficult step, provokes fear. Fear offers us the opportunity of fight or flight. Physiologically, this induces either weakening of the muscles – corresponding to flight – or excessive tension, depriving the muscles of freedom and looseness. In either case, the muscles do not work properly, and not a single step is possible. Fear is the cause of stage fright. One cannot eliminate it entirely – it is a natural phenomenon; to a greater or lesser extent, everyone feels fear at compromising himself. A child should be prepared for the fact that his artistic life will be composed of similarly stressful situations every single day. If every performance is going to be a great drama, an experience associated with enormous fear every single time, then psychiatric help will eventually be necessary. The point is to develop in the child an ability to concentrate on the tasks he is performing and to teach him to have the right attitude towards performance. His concentration must be focused on what he is doing, not on who is looking at him at any given moment, or on how they are judging him. The pleasure and joy which a healthy body finds in movement – in dance – should be so absorbing and so total that the public does not really have any influence on the dancing. The dancer should not be looking for approval as if in a mirror – in this case the audience – but rather, everything he does should flow from inside, it should all be an expression of his inner image of the dance, his inner concentration, co-ordination and aesthetic of movement, the source of his emotional experiences, his musical sensitivity and ability to make use of various means of expression. If a dancer could involve one half of his brain in the mechanics of movement and the other half in the creative ecstasy of dance, he would achieve the ideal state.

The dance world in the West today

Today's dance world is concentrated in three main centres – New York, London and Paris; next some other great cities, then all the rest. It may seem curious that an enormous number of dancers prefer to be on the dole in the great centres such as New York, rather then get involved in small centres. However, it is understandable since, even if they are dying of hunger, they are still close to Broadway, the three most important ballet companies in the United States, dozens of lesser companies and television, and thus never far away from the chance of finding the work they dream of. At the same time, they are witness to the entire spectrum of musical, theatrical and dancing life. In this chapter, I shall limit myself to some comments on the subject of New York dancers and teachers, as I worked in that city for three years – first as a teacher at Carnegie Hall, West Side School of Ballet and 'Steps', then as a guest teacher at the Joffrey Ballet and finally as ballet master at American Ballet Theatre – and know the New York environment very well.

The American Ballet Theatre usually starts a three- or four-month tour of the States at the beginning of December after a two-to-three month rehearsal period. The company performs six days in each city, giving eight performances in all, since they dance two shows on Wednesdays and Saturdays. They usually fly between cities on Sunday afternoons, and have Mondays free. From the very start of the tour right through to the end (the end of April), when the nine-to-thirteen week season begins in New York, two to three weeks can be set aside for rehearsals. By June, at the end of the season, the dancer will have 180 performances behind him; he is obliged contractually to do six hours of rehearsals a day.

A friend of mine who was acting and dancing the leading role in a musical on Broadway appeared eight times a week from June 1983 to May 1984, that is, about 360 times altogether. There were three musical scenes in the show, lasting about 20 minutes each.

In view of the great physical effort and crazy nervous stress (only the success of last night's performance counts), the instinct for self-preservation dictates a certain way of life, which forces the dancers to find their own rhythm of work and rest, a suitable diet and a suitable choice of training.

Since company directors aren't interested in how much and where the dancers exercise (company classes are not obligatory and are not counted in the
number of working hours) but only in how well they are dancing today, the
dancers' form from day to day is their own responsibility. New York, a city
of contrasts like every great metropolis, has a very large number of schools
and centres of varying quality, methods, styles and standards of teaching. As
in every sphere of life, all the best and all the worst are there for the taking,
so the choice depends purely on the dancer's discernment and financial
means. That's why there are so many dancers in the city with extremely varied training, and studios advertising themselves as teaching the methods of
Vaganova, Cecchetti, Legat, the English Royal Academy of Dancing, and so
on. In the States, the only company unique in its technical training is the
New York City Ballet, where the overwhelming majority of dancers come
from the School of American Ballet. This school has a teaching system established by George Balanchine, and disburses a large number of grants. Its aim
is to prepare pupils for the neoclassical style of the New York City Ballet repertoire. This style is characterised by high-precision footwork, unbelievable
speed, athletic energy, a particular kind of musicality and a slightly noncha-
lant port de bras. Classes in this style are extremely difficult for novices because of their fast tempo.

   To keep up competition, the teachers at dozens of other schools offer
the dancer a variety of individual approaches, and it is up to him to decide
who can really give him the best help with his work on stage. As usual, above
all it is a matter of finding a way to gain the maximum effect for the minimum effort. At most schools the classes are divided into four levels: beginners, mature amateurs, child beginners, and advanced and professionals. The
ideal teacher (thus a different one for each individual), assuming that professional dancers who attend classes already know how to dance, tries in a logical manner and in harmony with the dancer's anatomical build, to identify,
stimulate and strengthen whichever muscles he needs to work on most.

   Even visiting dancers from the provinces know the names of the most
popular teachers in New York: Stanley Williams teaches at the School of
American Ballet and is largely responsible for training many of the dancers at

52

the New York City Ballet and other companies, to achieve their phenomenal speed, the precision of their footwork and their exceptional turn-out. During the long two-hour sessions given by the Briton David Howard, the studio is bursting with dancers from the American Ballet Theatre and Broadway. He is their favourite, since his healthy, sensible and gentle method enables them to keep their muscles fit for battle in a relatively painless way. Maggie Black, who was my chosen teacher, is the slowest in tempo and has faithful followers among soloists of the American Ballet Theatre and the Joffrey Ballet. Her no-nonsense method, in which everything is well thought-out and logical, forces one to use not just muscles, but also the brain. I believe her idea of repeating short, simple exercises at the barre twice is excellent; the first time they are done at a slow tempo, the second time at a fast one, so that the first time you think, the second time you simply do. All the best teachers develop a vocabulary of classical dance through inventing additional exercises which enable one to achieve specific results. They all try to help the dancer by making him aware of his individual shortcomings and needs.

Sometimes one of the factors which determines the dancer's choice of one lesson rather than another may be the personality of the accompanying pianist, particularly if it is of the quality of the late superstar of the classroom, Lynn Stanford. He is remembered among dance professionals all over the world through his cassette recordings, and has become their favourite. His energy, wit, imagination and especially his ability to find the appropriate dynamic accents mean that a musical dancer quite simply cannot perform the given step incorrectly.

In this area another element has appeared which has a promising future in the development of classical dance technique – co-operation with rehabilitation centres. These centres employ kinesiotherapists and have lately been literally besieged by dancers. The kinesiotherapist recommends exercises using equipment which can strengthen just about every group of muscles, which help to compensate for particular shortcomings and eliminate weak points – in a word, perfecting and replenishing the dancer's toolbox. Since lessons at these centres are very expensive, more and more new gadgets have been appearing on the market; lightweight, ingenious little devices which

53

dancers can buy for their own use and which travel with them on tour. It might be a flexible metal 'magic hoop', which when squeezed in the right way strengthens the inner and back thigh muscles, so very important in maintaining the outer rotation or turn-out. Or it might be a hoop made of strong flexible rubber, which when appropriately stretched or pulled helps one to improve supple extensions and strengthens the muscles of the feet, knees and thighs. The possibilities are endless, it merely depends on the imagination of the user.

The so-called 'floor barre' of modern and jazz dance, which borrows certain elements from yoga, is a therapeutic way to begin the dancing day as preparation for a classical dance class. Young men often attend gyms to strengthen the upper part of the body with weights, thus preparing themselves or keeping themselves in shape for pas de deux work. The American Ballet Theatre company even takes a slanting bench and a set of weights on tour together with the sets. During the vacation, which often lasts for two to four months – and is unpaid – few people stop exercising for any longer than two weeks. The majority treat this period as a time of particularly strenuous work (two or three classes a day) to make as much progress as possible in order to end in a more highly qualified group after the vacation. Famous, older, and more experienced dancers try to get a place in concert groups, festivals or teaching training courses for the young.

Lastly, there is the matter of diet. At about the age of twenty-five, some dancers start to become aware that their diet influences how they feel and the standard of their work. Dieticians the world over, who often have extremely varied opinions on the subject of what one should eat, agree on one point only: the secret of good condition and longevity is to eat the minimum amount of food with the maximum nutritional value. The average diet of the conscientious ballerina is breakfast consisting of some fruit, yoghurt, cereal and less often, eggs. At mid-day she has a salad, a sandwich or grilled dish, and her supper after the performance is again salad, vegetables and light proteins such as meat, fish or poultry. Since there are rarely any canteens at the places where rehearsals are held, one often sees perspiring girls eating carrot sticks, celery, yoghurts or apples. American dancers are distinct from other nationalities by their slenderness and great store of energy. Maybe this goes hand in hand with their dietary system?

East and West

Classical ballet technique was conceived, I believe, when all stages were built with a rake. On such a surface the stance has to be different from that on a level floor. That is, the upper body leans slightly back at the waist. This stance has become characteristic of the Russian dancers, as both the Maryinsky and Bolshoi Theatres and Schools have different, but rather steep rakes.

I believe that the development of the Soviet (Moscow) style with its broader, more generous and heroic arm movements encouraged further the role of the back as the source of their strength, as opposed to Petipa's style that was aristocratic, but restricted by the traditional boned corsetry.

I remember constant remarks from the Russian teachers 'Hold and use your back', 'No one ever fell backwards only on their noses', and so on. Natalia Makarova says in her biography that only in the West did she hear for the first time, 'Hold your stomach in'.

In the Russians' dancing there are so many different épaulements and constant bends in different directions, that without their exceptionally thorough training of the muscles throughout the entire spine, it is not possible to move as they do. This carriage of the back and beautifully open chest ends at the elbows to allow full freedom for the stunning, sinuous forearms and hands, relaxed neck and elegantly poised head, adding up to an image of unique aristocratic grace. I do not, however, find this stance particularly helpful for multiple pirouettes, especially on pointe.

In the States, where the stages are mostly level, the stance is more upright, and I would say the dancers balance themselves by using the stomach muscles and the turn-out from inside the pelvis (Russians simply open the legs to the side rather than scooping the head of the femur in the hip socket to gain maximum rotation American style). Last but not least, they use the strength of their feet.

The Paris Opéra stage is raked, but the French dancers with their magnificent technique seem to stand much straighter than the Russians. They are similar to the Americans in that their weight is on the balls of the toes. The French use their perfect turn-out and hip placement as the source of balance. However, their arms are more functional than expressive and their backs less involved in all épaulements than the Russians.

Mr B., who I would say shaped American taste in ballet, asked for a more contemporary use of the arms. They are more free (the classical positions are passed through but not held) and 'jazzy' with their undulating elbows and 'broken' wrists.

The sheer speed of Balanchine's choreography as well as his respect for the composer's tempi, usually excludes the big vertical jumps which are of such importance to Russian taste, using them instead to cover space. The tempo also dictates shorter preparations and speedier, earlier take-offs than the Russians. Hard floors discourage sitting in plié. Even dancers with exceptional ballon cannot stay airborne for too long or they are in danger of being late for the next step (Baryshnikov darted through the air in Balanchine ballets rather than hovering in it).

This also means that in the class, medium jumps – sissonne, for example – using the deep soft plié vital for soaring jumps, are omitted (because they do not dance them on stage), and the grand allegro is done at breakneck speed.

With the romantic ballets, or Petipa's choreography, the height of the jumps is very important, and even more the soft, silent landings. The Russian classes therefore have slower tempi for centre practice, a larger amount of fondus (vitally important in developing strong high jumps and controlled landings), développés, turns in big positions and a much longer and slower jumping section.

As a dancer I remember feeling caught between these different styles, finding it difficult to adjust to the slow Russian tempo and then to the speed of the Americans.

I believe that dancers in companies with a mixed repertoire (which for example includes ballets like *Giselle*, *La Bayadère* and *Symphony in C*) should be exposed to each approach, according to their current requirements. Probably the best solution would be to have guest teachers from the best sources who understand the dancers' needs, not only rehearsing the ballets but giving classes appropriate to the style and technique of the piece.

I have often been asked the question: 'Is it possible to combine American legwork and Russian épaulements, or do the two cancel one another out?' My first thought was of the Kirov-trained Elena Pankova in Balanchine's *Scotch Symphony*, a perfect marriage of Russian training and American-style choreography. Suzanne Farrell relates in her autobiography how keen Elena was to learn a style new to her and how hard she worked to achieve it. The Maryinsky troupe already has a few of Mr B.'s ballets in their repertoire and we may await the results with interest.

The question has larger implications to it however: when one is young and eager to learn, the 'unprogrammed computer' of one's brain generally registers the first information as the ideal, against which one compares other information at a later date. In other words, 'best' is what one has learnt first (isn't Mum's cooking always best?). One's entire aesthetic outlook has been shaped then, one's 'good taste'; like the 'best' versions of ballets, the 'best' construction of a class and so on. But only when one travels does one find that what was beautiful and in good taste in one's own country, is ugly and in bad taste in country B and totally irrelevant in country C.

I have often heard as an insult to a dancer 'you dance as if you were from such and such a company' (meaning of course a leading company).

One has to appreciate the beauty of other styles to be able to combine them. It is not possible to combine different styles, different aesthetics without the ability to see the beauty of both, accepting and admiring them equally.

Thanks to TV and video, some merging of ideas has already begun in spite of some opposition. However there is some evidence of the emergence of a homogenised 'all-purpose' style, whereas the contrary should apply. We must use the new technology sensitively and intelligently in order to develop our knowledge and application of the different styles and techniques of ballet.

Unfortunately I am afraid that the twenty-first century is coming with its computers and ballet 'robots'. 'They are here,' as the little girl in the film *Poltergeist* said. It would be an amusing game to try and guess how many of the important figures in ballet history would not even be accepted into the schools now, neither would they get a job. In all honesty, when was technique alone a passport to history?

As long as physical attributes are the priority – bulging insteps, hyper-extended flexibility and an overall deformed 'classical' line – as long as these are admired, wanted and cherished above qualities such as relaxed grace of the upper body, melting expressive arms, sensitivity to different styles and the ability to create a magical atmosphere on stage, embodying the music rather than simply keeping on the beat – we are really not progressing, are we? A rare example of dancer and music merging would be Koen Onzia in his final solo from Christopher Bruce's *Swansong*, the dancer engaging fully in the swell of the music and carrying the audience along with him.

But in general I feel we are in danger of losing the chance of seeing someone dancing so generously, larger-than-life, like Maya Plisetskaya in the first act of *Don Quixote* and *The Fountains of Bakhchisaray* or Gelsey Kirkland's chilling stillness in the mad scene from *Giselle*.

'Lasciate ogni speranza' we are up to our noses in the next century.

Technique and expression

It is an undeniable fact that the standard of classical dance technique, particularly in the last 15–20 years has risen considerably. Agility and purity of performance, once accessible only to a very few exceptional naturally gifted people, is becoming the property of an ever wider and younger generation. I believe we are still far from reaching the limits of what the human body can do, in keeping with physiology and the laws of nature. Concentration close to the level of that of Buddhist monks, awareness of the purpose of every movement, exercises which force the student to be constantly in control of the relationship between his centre of gravity and base of opposition, strengthening of muscles by repeating combinations of movements rather than making them more complex – these are the basic principles of modern classical dance teaching. One might imagine a pyramid of success which is built by a daily return to the basics, strengthening and expanding them. The broader the base, the higher one can reach, the stronger and longer one can stand. Of course, the mechanics of movement is only half the problem of training or keeping in shape for the professional dancer. Despite the fact that, in the final analysis, it is the strength of one's muscles which alone determines the movement which we see on stage, even the most fantastic technique, if it is without soul, makes the dance seem dry and empty. The role of the teacher-coach in the second half of the dancer's working day, in rehearsals and performance, is to help him to find himself as an individual, to help him to add life and meaning to every single step. If the mechanical side of the role has already been mastered, the dancer can concentrate on drawing a psychological portrait of the character he is dancing, reaching into his own life experience, sensitivity and creative imagination.

The balance between the physical and spiritual, muscle fitness and emotional subtext, the truth behind every single movement makes dance into an art which reflects life. Its ephemerality in time and space is a part of its glory and the elusive perfection must be endlessly sought after, as it exists only in the memory and in each successive performance.

Koen Onzia in Christopher Bruce's *Swansong.*   PHOTO: BILL COOPER

6

Ballet class

This is a sample ballet class designed for advanced students. 'Ballet Class 1', a recording of piano music to accompany this class played by Jonathan Still, is available on cassette (see back page for details).

BARRE

Cassette Side A

---

1. *Tendus from 1st position facing the barre*　　　*Music 2/4. Preparation 4 bars*
1 count = 1 bar

  1　　　　　　2　　3　　　4　　　5　　6　　7　　8
Tendu devant, flex, point, close. Repeat à la seconde.

  1　2　3　4　　　　　　　5　　　　　　　　　　6
2 demi-pliés, dégagé à la seconde with right leg, bring to turned-in retiré,

    7　　　　　　　8
turn out in retiré, close 1st position.

• Repeat all to the left then repeat in reverse.

---

2. *Tendus from 1st position, left hand on barre*　　　*Music 2/4. Preparation 2 bars*
1 count = 1 bar

  1　2　3　　　　　　　　　4　　　　5　6　7　8　　　　1　2　3　4
3 tendus devant (accent out), demi-plié. Repeat à la seconde and inside leg devant.

   5　　　6　　　7　　　8
Port de bras forward with feet parallel.

• Reverse (with port de bras back).

61

3. Pliés

   1   2   3   4   5 6 7 8
2 demi-pliés in 2nd position, 1 grand plié,

   1   2   3   4   5 6 7   & 8
port de bras towards the barre and away, tendu to 1st position.

  1—8   1   2   3   4   5 6 7   & 8
Same plié, port de bras forward and back, tendu to 4th position.

  1 2 3 4   5   6   7   8
2 demi-pliés, port de bras towards pointed foot devant (left leg en fondu), recover,

     1   2   3   4
temps lié en avant, port de bras back, recover,

     5   6   7
relevé balance in 4th position, lower heels,

          8
tendu left foot derrière and close to 5th position,

   1 2 3 4   5   6   7   8
2 demi-pliés, 1 grand plié in 5th,

   1 2 3 4 5 6   7   8
circular port de bras, relevé balance in 5th position.

• Other side.

4. Tendus from 5th position (slow tempo)

   1   2   3   4
Tendu devant (accent out), close 5th position, demi-plié, straighten,

   5   6   7 8
demi-plié, small pas de cheval devant to pointe tendue, 2 tendus devant (accent in).

Repeat en croix.

   1   2   3   4   5   6   7   8
2 tendus à la seconde right leg (accent out), 2 tendus à la seconde left leg (accent out)

$\overset{1}{}\quad\overset{2}{}\quad\overset{3}{}\quad\overset{4}{}$
2 demi-pliés in 5th position

$\overset{5}{}\quad\overset{6}{}\quad\overset{7}{}\quad\overset{8}{}$
1 slow retiré, close 5th position right leg derrière.

Reverse from two tendus à la seconde.

• Other side.

5. *Tendus from 5th position (medium tempo)*   *Music 3/4. Preparation 4 bars*
1 count = 1 bar

$\overset{1}{}\qquad\overset{2}{}\qquad\overset{3}{}\qquad\qquad\overset{4}{}$
3 tendus devant (accent in) with last to demi-plié, tendu devant

$\overset{5}{}\qquad\qquad\qquad\overset{6}{}$
lower heel to 4th position, point front foot,

$\overset{7}{}\qquad\qquad\qquad\qquad\overset{\&}{}\qquad\overset{8}{}$
lower heel to 4th position demi-plié, point front foot, close in 5th position.

Repeat en croix.

• Other side.

6. *Tendus in 5th position (fast tempo)*   *Music 2/4. Preparation 2 bars*
2 counts = 1 bar

$\overset{1}{}\ \overset{2}{}\ \overset{3}{}\ \overset{4}{}\qquad\qquad\overset{5}{}\qquad\overset{6}{}\ \overset{7}{}\ \overset{8}{}$
5 tendus devant (accent in), last one to demi-plié, straighten.

$\overset{1-8}{}\qquad\qquad\overset{1-8}{}\qquad\qquad\overset{1-8}{}$
Repeat à la seconde and inside leg devant. Port de bras forward.

Reverse (with port de bras back).

• Other side.

7. *Glissés from 5th position (medium tempo)*   *Music 3/4. Preparation 4 bars*
1 count = 1 bar

              &   *1*
Draw the foot through cou-de-pied, close to 1st position,

     &   *2*   *&* *3* *&* *4*
repeat, close 5th position finish derrière, repeat in reverse finishing 5th position devant,

     5   *6*   *7* *8*
développé devant (45°), 2 glissés (accent in).

Repeat en croix.

• Other side.

Alternative version:

   1   *2*   *3* *4*   *5*   *6*   *7* *8*
Développé devant (45°), 2 glissés, 1 piqué, 1 enveloppé to 5th position in plié.

Repeat en croix.

8. *Glissés from 5th position (fast tempo)*   *Music 2/4. Preparation 2 bars*
2 counts = 1 bar

   1   *2*   *3*   *4*
2 glissés devant, 2 glissés à la seconde (closing derrière, devant)

   5   *6* *7* *8*
retiré right leg, lower to 5th position right leg derrière.

Reverse.

   1 *2*   *3*   *4*
4 battements en cloche (open on 'and' to the devant position),

   5   *6*   *7*   *8*
passer through cou-de-pied to low arabesque, close 5th position derrière,

   1   *2*   *3*   *4*
3 glissés in 1st position à la seconde, close 5th position devant.

5   6   7   8
3 glissés in 1st position à la seconde, close 5th position derrière.

Reverse.

• Other side.

9. *Ronds de jambe à terre*   *Music 3/4. Preparation 4 bars*
1 count = 1 bar

1   2
1 slow rond de jambe en dehors with supporting leg in fondu
(straightening supporting leg during rond de jambe),

3   4
2 ronds de jambe en dehors,

5   6   7   8
battement devant (45°), flex foot and rond to low arabesque, point foot,

1   2   3   4
3 ronds de jambe en dehors, battement to attitude devant en fondu (90°),

5   6
rond to side straightening supporting leg, rond attitude derrière en fondu,

7   8
straighten both legs to arabesque, brush through 1st position to pointe tendue devant.

Reverse.

1 2 3 4   5
Circular port de bras (away from the barre), tendu left foot derrière,

6   7   8   1 2   3 4
lunge to big 4th position, recover, bend back, recover,

5   6   7   8
draw both legs to 5th position on demi-pointe, retiré right leg, balance.

• Other side.

10. *Fondus*   *Music 2/4. Preparation 2 bars*
                                        2 counts = 1 bar

     1   *2*   *3*
Fondu devant, fondu in attitude devant,

         4
rond de jambe à la seconde straightening both legs.

    5   *6*   *7*   *8*
Repeat from à la seconde to arabesque.

    1   *2*
Fondu inside leg (left) devant,

       3   *4*
fondu working leg keeping raised leg extended, relevé,

    5   *6*   *7* *8*
bring left leg to 5th position, retiré left leg, balance.

Reverse and repeat on demi-pointe.

• Other side.

Alternatively, for tired legs, turn to the other side and do the exerise on flat foot. Turn again and repeat on demi-pointe.

11. *Frappés*   *Music 2/4. Preparation 2 bars*
                                        2 counts = 1 bar

   1 2 3   *&*   *4*   *5 6 7 8*   *1 2 3 4*
3 frappés devant, flex, point. Repeat à la seconde and derrière.

    5   *6* *7*   *8*
1 double frappé en croix (starting à la seconde and finishing derrière).

Reverse.

   1   *2*   *3 4*
Close to demi-plié in 5th position right foot devant, relevé,

    5   6   7   8   1—8
développé à la seconde (45°), balance.

• Other side.

12. *Ronds de jambe en l'air*   *Music 3/8. Preparation 4 bars*
                                                    1 count = 1 bar

    1   2   3
Battement devant (90°), enveloppé to retiré on demi-pointe,

    4
close 5th position right leg devant.

    5   6   7   8
Repeat with inside leg to arabesque.

        1   2   3   4
Battement à la seconde, 3 ronds de jambe en dehors,

  5 6 7   8
retiré balance close 5th position right leg derrière.

Reverse.

    1—8   1—6   7   8
Circular port de bras en dedans and en dehors, relevé in 5th position.

• Other side.

13. *Adagio*   *Music 4/4. Preparation 2 bars*
                                                2 counts = 1 bar

    1 2 3   4   5   6   7   8
Développé devant, close 5th position. Repeat to arabesque with the inside leg (left).

    1   2   3   4   5
Développé à la seconde with right leg, passer retiré, développé devant en fondu,

    6   7
grand rond de jambe to arabesque (progressively straightening the standing leg),

close 5th position derrière.

Reverse.

• Other side.

14. Petits battements

Music 2/4. Preparation 4 bars
1 count = 1 bar

1 fondu à la seconde (45°), 2 doubles ronds de jambe en l'air en dehors (45°),

petits battements sur le cou-de-pied, finish à la seconde.

Reverse and repeat all on demi-pointe.

Coupé over to fondu left leg cou-de-pied, pointe tendue derrière,

deep lunge with port de bras forward, recover to 5th position demi-pointe,

développé inside leg to attitude derrière, balance.

• Other side.

15. Grands battements

Music 3/4. Preparation 4 bars
1 count = 1 bar

2 grands battements devant (accent up), repeat à la seconde,

4 battements en cloche starting devant (accent up),

2 grands ronds de jambe jetés en dehors, close 5th position back
(brush through 1st position to small attitude devant and throw leg in an arc
to pointe tendue derrière with the maximum high point in écarté back).

Reverse.

• Other side.

16. **Stretch** *Music 12/8. Preparation 4 bars.*

CENTRE

1. Tendus

Music 2/4. Preparation 4 bars
1 count = 1 bar

     1   *2*   *3*   *4*
3 tendus croisés devant (accent in), last one to demi-plié, tendu croisé devant,

     5   *6*
temps lié through 4th position in demi-plié to pointe tendue back,

     7   *8*
temps lié back through demi-pointe, close 5th position.

     1—8   *1—8*
Repeat with the right leg à la seconde and croisé back.

                               1   *2*   *3*   *4*   *5 6*
(From tendu croisé back) deep lunge to 4th position, bend forward, back

     7   *8*
recover up to tendu croisé back, close 5th position.

• Repeat to the left.

2. Adagio

Music 3/4. Preparation 4 bars
1 count = 1 bar

     1   *2*   *3*   *4*
Grand plié in 2nd position, tendu right leg and close 5th position devant,

     5   *6*   *7*   *8*
développé right leg to écarté derrière, close 5th position croisé right leg derrière,

     1   *2*   *3*   *4*
développé with the left leg croisé devant, passé to attitude croisé derrière,

     5   *6*
fondu allongé to arabesque,

     7   *8*
pas de bourrée under to 5th position, left leg croisé devant to finish.

• Repeat to the left.

3. Pirouettes en dehors

1   2
Tendu right leg à la seconde, demi-plié in 2nd position,

3   4
relevé onto the left leg with the right in retiré, close 5th position right leg devant,

5   6   &
tendu right leg à la seconde, rond de jambe derrière, demi-plié in 4th position,

7   8
relevé with right leg in retiré, close 5th position right leg devant.

1   2   3   4
1 pirouette en dehors from 5th position, close derrière, tendu à la seconde or derrière,

5   6   7   &   8
pirouettes from 2nd or 4th position, finish 4th position croisé, recover to 5th position.

• Repeat to the left.

4. Fondus

1   2   3   4
Fondu right leg à la seconde, 2 ronds de jambe en l'air en dehors,

&
close 5th position right leg derrière, fondu left leg à la seconde,   5   6

7   8   1   2
2 ronds de jambe en l'air en dehors, bring leg to passé on demi-pointe,

3   4
close 5th position left leg croisé derrière, tendu right leg croisé devant,

&   5   6
tombé to 4th position, pirouettes en dedans in retiré position,

7   8
close 5th position left leg devant.

• Repeat to the left. Repeat 2nd time with turns en dedans in attitude.

5. Grands battements

    1   *2*
Grand battement right leg (accent up) devant in effacé,

    3   *4*
grand battement right leg à la seconde en face (closing right leg derrière),

    5   *6*   *&*
relevé in 1st arabesque in effacé right leg up, tombé over, coupé under

    7 8
2 balancés (right then left),

    1   *2*
tombé pas de bourrée effacé devant to the right to 5th position left leg devant,

    3   *4*
tendu preparation with right leg derrière to 4th position plié,

    5   *6*   *7*   *8*
pirouettes en dehors in retiré, finish 5th position croisé, right leg derrière.

• Repeat to the left.

Advanced alternative:

    1   *2*
Grand battement piqué croisé devant, (right leg opening on 'and'),

    3   *4*
grand battement piqué croisé derrière (left leg),

    1   *2*   *3*   *4*
grand battement piqué à la seconde (right leg), repeat with the left leg,

       1   *2*
tendu croisé right leg devant, tombé 4th position,

     3   *4*
pirouette en dedans à la seconde or arabesque (to the right),

     5   *6*   *7*   *8*
fondu on supporting leg, soutenu en dedans, plié, glissade over.

ALLEGRO

1. Small jumps from two feet

Music 2/4. Preparation 4 bars
1 count = 1 bar

Start 5th position right foot devant.

    1 2 3 4   5 6 7 8
4 sautés in 1st position, 4 sautés in 2nd position,

       1   *2   3   4*
close to 5th position right leg derrière, 3 changements de pied,

    5   *6*   *7*   *8*
jump to 2nd position, straighten, plié in 2nd, jump to 5th position changing legs.

• Repeat.

2. Assemblés

Music 3/4; 3/8. Preparation 4 bars
1 count = 1 bar

Start 5th position left foot devant.

  1   *2*   *3*   *4*
2 assemblés over (right and left), glissade, assemblé over to the right,

   5
sissonne ouverte à la seconde to the left (right leg opens to 45°),

  &   *6*
coupé under, ballonné left leg à la seconde (finishing left foot cou-de-pied back),

  & *7*   *8*
coupé tombé to 4th position croisé, assemblé left leg croisé back.

• Repeat to the left.

Alternative version to 2nd melody (all travelling to the right):

 1   *2*   *3 4 5 6* *7*   *8*
Assemblé over, sissonne over, repeat twice, glissade derrière, assemblé over,

 1—8
repeat travelling to the left.

3. Jetés

Start 5th position, right foot devant.

     1   *2*   *3*   *4*
Jeté over, temps levé in cou-de-pied position (repeat left),

     5   *6*   *7* *8*
glissade derrière, jeté over (repeat left),

    1   *2*   *3*   *4*
coupé ballonné under (left and right),

     5   *6*
coupé under, rond de jambe en l'air sauté, finishing left leg extended effacé devant,

                          7   *8*
step forward, brush through right leg and assemblé croisé devant.

• Repeat to the left.

4. Batterie

Start 5th position, right foot devant.

   1   *2*   *3*   *4*   *5*   *6*
2 entrechats quatre, 1 échappé, 2 brisés travelling effacé en avant to the right,

    7   *8*
sissonne ouverte in 2nd arabesque, pas de bourrée under.
(All travelling to the right)

• Repeat to the left.

Then repeat faster.

5. Sissonnes

Start 5th position, left foot devant.

   1   *2*
2 sissonnes fermées in 1st arabesque to effacé right,

   3
sissonne ouverte in attitude croisée (right leg in attitude),

  &   *4*
coupé under, assemblé croisé devant,

  5   *6*   *&* *7*   *8*
tombé pas de bourrée effacé to the left, relevé, plié, entrechat six.

• Repeat to the left.

6. Grand allegro from upstage left corner

Start with left leg tendu devant croisé.

  1   *2*
Glissade assemblé entrechat six de volée, finishing with right leg devant,

  3
step back with left leg croisé and relevé développé right leg croisé devant (45°),

  4   *5*   *6*
pas couru, grand jeté in attitude croisé,

    7   *8*
piqué in 1st arabesque effacée, pas couru back along same diagonal,

  1   *2*   *3* *4*
grand jeté entrelacé (en tournant), pas couru forward, assemblé en tournant,

    5   *6*   *&*   *7*   *8*
Girls: tombé pas de bourrée to the left, glissade flick jeté in 1st arabesque.

    5   *6*   *&*   *7* *8*
Boys: tombé pas de bourrée to the left, assemblé left leg derrière, tour en l'air.

7. Coda (medium tempo)

For girls, on the diagonal:

    1   *2*   *3*   *4*
2 soutenus en tournant, 2 lame-ducks,

     5   *6*   *7 8*
2 piqués en dedans, chaînés, finish in tendu left leg effacé derrière.

Alternative: fouettés.

For boys, upstage right corner 3 times:

    1   *2*   *3*   *4*
Tombé pas de bourrée, assemblé left leg back, tour en l'air to 5th position or 4th position or 1st arabesque,

     5   *6*   *7*   *8*
then tendu side or back, pirouettes en dehors in passé position finish in 4th position or on the knee left leg croisé derrière.

Alternative: grandes pirouettes.

8. Coda (slower tempo)

Manège

Girls:

    1 *2*   *3*   *4*
2 piqués en dedans, tombé coupé jeté en tournant in 1st arabesque,

    5   *6*   *7 8*
2 piqués en dedans, chaînés.

Repeat.

Boys:

         1   *2*   *3*   *4*   *5—8*
3 times: 2 coupés jetés en tournant, tombé coupé 'barrel turn', chaînés.

9. *Port de bras in 1st position*

Music 4/4. Preparation 4 bars
1 count = 1 bar

     1   *2*   *3*   *4*
Port de bras sideways to the left,

     5   *6*   *7*   *8*
port de bras sideways to the right,

     1   *2*   *3*   *4*
circular port de bras to the right,

     5   *6*   *7*   *8*
relevé in 1st position.

• Repeat to the left.

'Ballet Class 1', a 75-minute digitally recorded cassette
tape of piano music played by Jonathan Still to accompany
the class given in this book, is available from:

Dance Books Ltd, 15 Cecil Court, London WC2N 4EZ.
Tel: 0171-836 2314. Fax: 0171-497 0473.